T0104264

# DEADLY HEARTS

## HISTORY'S MOST DANGEROUS PEOPLE

*To the next generation of my nieces
and nephews—may they never know
what it's like to live under a tyrant—MB*

## W

PENGUIN WORKSHOP
An imprint of Penguin Random House LLC, New York

First published in the United States of America by Penguin Workshop,
an imprint of Penguin Random House LLC, New York, 2022

Text copyright © 2022 by Penguin Random House LLC
Illustrations copyright © 2022 by Karl James Mountford

Visit us online at penguinrandomhouse.com.

Library of Congress Cataloging-in-Publication Data is available.

Manufactured in China

ISBN 9780593386675                    10 9 8 7 6 5 4 3 2 1 TOPL

Design by Julia Rosenfeld

# DEADLY HEARTS

## HISTORY'S MOST DANGEROUS PEOPLE

BY MICHAEL BURGAN
ILLUSTRATED BY KARL JAMES MOUNTFORD

PENGUIN WORKSHOP

# CONTENTS

INTRODUCTION 3

ALEXANDER THE GREAT (356 BCE–323 BCE) 9

JULIUS CAESAR (100 BCE–44 BCE) 17

ATTILA THE HUN (CA. 406–453 CE) 25

GENGHIS KHAN (CA. 1162–1227) 33

TOMÁS DE TORQUEMADA (1420–1498) 41

VLAD THE IMPALER (CA. 1431–CA. 1477) 49

HERNÁN CORTÉS (1485–1547) 57

QUEEN MARY I OF ENGLAND (1516–1558) 65

IVAN THE TERRIBLE (1530–1584) 73

ELIZABETH BÁTHORY (1560–1614) 81

MAXIMILIEN ROBESPIERRE (1758–1794) 89

QUEEN RANAVALONA I OF MADAGASCAR (1778–1861) 97

KING LEOPOLD II OF BELGIUM (1835–1909) 105

ADOLF HITLER (1889–1945) 113

IDI AMIN DADA (CA. 1925–2003) 121

POL POT (1925–1998) 129

SELECT BIBLIOGRAPHY 137

# INTRODUCTION

His body tied to a wooden rack, a man screams and begs for his life. Spanish soldiers tighten the ropes attached to his arms and legs. They stretch the man's body until he confesses to a crime he didn't commit— or until he dies.

In another part of Europe, wooden poles stick out of the ground, their tops sharpened to points. Just below one point, a body lies limp. With the pole piercing his body, the victim dies a slow death.

In Africa, piles of severed hands surround a military officer from Belgium. The soldiers under his command cut the hands from the bodies of rebels they kill, to prove they have not wasted any bullets. One hand means one bullet fired.

These gruesome scenes could have come from a horror movie. But they all actually happened. The deeds described here were carried out under the orders of ruthless people whose actions reflect the evil that humans are capable of.

Over centuries and around the world, there have been leaders with great power who have used cruelty and violence to get what they wanted. Some sought to conquer other lands so they could build great empires and amass personal wealth. Other leaders wanted to squash any threats to their rule from rebels or outside enemies. A few may have been driven by a touch of madness. Some people believed their god, or gods, had chosen them to rule and had given them a divine right to kill in the name of their religions. And some, for reasons that are hard for most people to understand, simply enjoyed seeing others suffer.

Collected here are the stories of sixteen men and women, powerful people with deadly hearts. What forces shaped them? Some lived when violence and cruelty seemed to be just a part of life—and rulers were expected to get what they wanted. Others believed that mass killing was an acceptable way to take revenge in response to harm done to them or their people.

Whatever their background or the world they faced, these sixteen people remind us that human nature has a dark side that can be unleashed in truly terrible ways. Their stories demonstrate that there is a long history of ruthless people who have wreaked havoc to get what they want. They might also say something about us, the people who are drawn to read about their horrible deeds. Do we read them to try to understand how some people can become so evil? Or perhaps to learn lessons we'd like to never see repeated?

Whether empire building or simply displaying a cruel streak, is there any excuse for the actions of people who have been responsible for the deaths of so many? And can we, as a society, prevent the rise of new "deadly hearts"? Or will the impulse for evil in some people always find a way out?

# ALEXANDER THE GREAT
## (356 BCE–323 BCE)

Royal rulers can often trace their family histories back to many kings. Alexander the Great made an even bolder claim: that through his father, his roots went back to the ancient Greek hero Heracles (often known as Hercules today). He, in turn, was the son of the most powerful of all the Greek gods, Zeus. On his mother's side, Alexander's family tree included the famous Greek warrior Achilles. Alexander did not deny stories that said his true father was the god Zeus himself!

With that background, it's no wonder that

Alexander the Great believed he was meant to accomplish great things. And he did—during his short life, he created one of the largest empires the world has ever seen. But along with skillfully commanding his troops, Alexander often showed a cruel and ruthless side.

His real father was not a god but King Philip II. Philip laid the foundation for Alexander's military success. As the king of Macedonia, one of several independent states located in what is now the nation of Greece, Philip expanded his country's army and made his soldiers professionals who pledged their loyalty to him. The Macedonians valued bravery on the battlefield, and the sons of noble families began training for military careers when they were fourteen years old.

Starting during the 350s BCE, Philip used his army to conquer Greek lands south of Macedonia and unite them under his rule. He was off fighting in 356 BCE when Alexander was born in the Macedonian capital of Pella. The young prince quickly showed that he had a sharp mind, and as a teenager he left Pella to study with the great Greek philosopher Aristotle.

One of the books Alexander read was the *Iliad*. It told the tales of Greek warriors in ancient times, and Alexander thought it was a very good guide on how to wage war against a nation's enemies. The book also showed Alexander that revenge could be a powerful force in world affairs. In the *Iliad*, a great war starts when the Greeks seek to retaliate against the city of Troy.

Revenge also drove Achilles, one of those warriors who is mentioned in the *Iliad*. After the death of one of his friends, Achilles sought out and killed the Trojan who had killed him.

Alexander's own mother, Olympias, may have led him to believe that Achilles was a distant relative of theirs. Alexander knew he was expected to follow in the footsteps of Achilles and other heroic soldiers of the past. Olympias may have also fed Alexander's belief that he was related to the gods—an idea that would have made him think he could do what he pleased when he became king.

Alexander also had a military role model close at hand—his father. Philip's wars against Greek cities continued as Alexander grew up. The boy once told friends that he was afraid his father would achieve so many victories, there would be nothing left for Alexander to do to show his greatness.

Although he had limited training in actual combat, Alexander commanded cavalry (soldiers on horseback) for his father when he was eighteen. But not all the violence Alexander experienced came on the battlefield. In 336 BCE, King Philip II was killed by a friend. It was said that Alexander's mother may have encouraged the murder, as she wanted her son Alexander to rule Macedonia in Philip's place.

The violence surrounding the royal family continued after Philip's death. To guarantee that he would become king, Alexander killed at least one of his own half brothers and others who might oppose his rule. Then, one of Philip's generals threw his support to Alexander, ensuring that he would take the throne. At the time, he was just twenty years old.

The Greek city of Thebes rebelled against the young king. Alexander took brutal revenge. One ancient historian noted that by the end of the fighting, "every corner of the city was piled high with corpses." Then Alexander carried off the city's children and enslaved them.

Once Alexander had full control of Greece, he led his army eastward. His target: Persia, at the time the largest empire in the world. The Persians had earlier invaded Greece and destroyed the city of Athens. As ruler of a united Greece, Alexander wanted revenge. Defeating the Persians would also bring him great wealth and glory.

In 334 BCE, Alexander and his army began their march through Persian lands, including what is now Turkey, Egypt, and Israel. The site of one of Alexander's worst acts of cruelty was in Tyre, an island city off the coast of Lebanon. To build a road over the water to attack the city, Alexander destroyed homes so that he could use their stone and wood. When the fighting was over, Alexander killed the city's rulers as well as thousands of soldiers who had survived the battle.

By 330 BCE, Alexander had reached the Persian capital of Persepolis. Persian troops were on the way to defend the city, but Alexander got there first. He let his men run wild through Persepolis, robbing and killing civilians. Alexander then burned the city's palaces.

After conquering the heart of Persia, Alexander continued to head east. His army fought and won in what is now Afghanistan, Uzbekistan, Tajikistan, and Pakistan. Their march of conquest finally ended in India. Along the way, Alexander captured and destroyed dozens of cities. As in Tyre, he often killed surrendering soldiers. Many civilians died in the fighting as well. Alexander was known for savage bouts of anger, which he directed at his enemies. When one Persian governor refused to accept his authority, Alexander had him tied to the back of a chariot and dragged through the city.

Some of his anger and the resulting violence might have been fueled by alcohol, as Alexander was a heavy drinker. After one night of drinking, he argued with Cleitus, one of his top generals, and drove a spear through Cleitus's chest. And Alexander killed others close to him if he suspected he was losing their loyalty.

At times, the Macedonian king may have used the sudden bursts of violence to frighten his enemies. But his cruel streak suggested that some of his behavior was not part of a grand military plan. At one battle, his enemy hired some seven thousand soldiers to fight the Greeks. After Alexander won, he agreed to let these hired soldiers be released. But then he changed his mind and had them all killed.

By 326 BCE, after being away for almost ten years, Alexander's men wanted to return home, and he agreed. But the great conqueror would not see Pella again. He died in 323 BCE in what is now Iraq. Some people at the time thought he might have been poisoned. Modern theories suggest he could have died from alcoholism or another disease.

To some, Alexander was a great leader because of his military successes. He also spread Greek culture to parts of Asia, where his influence is still felt. Some boys are still named Iskander, an Arab version of "Alexander." And at least one figure from Greek myth, Heracles, appears in Buddhist writings. But in his drive to build his vast empire, and at times take revenge on others, Alexander also killed tens of thousands of innocent people.

# JULIUS CAESAR
## (100 BCE–44 BCE)

A famous quote from ancient Rome is still sometimes repeated today: *Veni vidi vici*. That Latin phrase means "I came, I saw, I conquered," and its author was Julius Caesar, a Roman general and political leader. His dream was to rule all of Rome, and he hoped his military victories would ensure his fame and win support of the Romans. His victories, though, came at the cost of many innocent lives.

From a tiny village along Italy's Tiber River, Rome grew to become a powerful military force. By the time Gaius Julius Caesar was born in 100 BCE,

Rome controlled all of Italy and parts of Spain, France, Greece, North Africa, and Turkey.

For Roman generals, victory in foreign lands meant praise back in Rome. The most successful generals used their popularity—and the wealth they won from conquering others—to gain political power, in addition to the military power they already had. Julius Caesar followed that path after his successful battles in Gaul. That region included most of France and parts of Belgium and other nearby countries. Gaul is also where Caesar earned his reputation as a ruthless killer, slaughtering hundreds of thousands of people.

But who was Caesar? His family said they could trace their roots to Aeneas, an ancient Roman hero. Though Caesar belonged to the ruling class of Romans, he did not have great wealth. He did, however, have intelligence, a talent for public speaking, and a knack for making friends with rich and powerful Romans.

During Caesar's youth, Rome faced trouble from within and from outside forces. In Italy, Romans fought a civil war over who should rule. In what is now Turkey, enemy forces invaded land in the region under Roman control.

During the civil war, several of Caesar's relatives were killed. While still a teen, he faced the possibility of death himself. His name was on a list of people who were considered enemies of Sulla, Rome's dictator during the early 80s BCE. The people who ended up on his enemies list could lose their property—or their lives. For a time, Caesar had to flee Rome to save his life. The warfare and political battles within Rome may have convinced the young Caesar that his country needed a strong ruler to survive.

Like many Roman men who were of noble backgrounds but had little money, Caesar joined the army. He showed great skill on the battlefield. Thanks to his political connections, he won several government positions, and in 61 BCE he went to Spain to serve as its governor. He led troops against Spanish tribes who were resisting Roman rule. During his time as governor there, Caesar amassed great wealth, and he used some of his money to pay his soldiers. With that and his military talents, he won their loyalty.

He also won the support of some of the poorer people of Rome. When he was in the city, he spent money on public entertainment. He also spoke out at times against the wealthy men who controlled Roman politics. Like Alexander the Great before him, Caesar claimed to have family ties to the gods. He was paving the way for others to see him as a great man bound to rule.

By 59 BCE, Caesar's power was certainly on the rise. He shared control of the Roman government with two other men, Pompey and Crassus. He governed several Roman provinces, or territories, including the part of Gaul west of the Alps. Most of the land was not under direct Roman control. Caesar seized on the chance to extend Roman rule through conquest. That, he knew, would only increase his influence in Rome.

Caesar started what are known as the Gallic Wars in 58 BCE. His first target was a tribe called the Helvetians. Commanding an army of up to thirty thousand men, he pursued them across the Saône River in what is now eastern France. Most of the Helvetians made it across the river before Caesar's troops reached them, but about a quarter did not. The Helvetians included women and children, and Caesar attacked them along with the soldiers. The women and children tried to defend themselves, but as a Roman historian noted, they "were cut to pieces with the men."

The fighting in Gaul went on for almost a decade, with Caesar also venturing into Britain and lands along the Rhine River. The Gauls, on the whole, were familiar with warfare and could be brutal themselves. Their warriors sometimes hung the severed heads of their enemies on their doorways! But the slaughter Caesar carried out in Gaul was on a huge scale.

Fighting German tribes along the Rhine and Meuse Rivers, Caesar ordered his men to chase and kill fleeing women and children. The German soldiers saw this and realized they would be attacked, so they retreated, but they could not escape the Romans. Caesar's men killed about four hundred thousand people during this single battle.

Caesar was also responsible for what we know today as genocide. That means the mass killing of people of one ethnic or racial background. Caesar's act of genocide came against the Eburones. This tribe from northeastern Gaul had earlier carried out a successful sneak attack against Caesar's troops. In 53 BCE, Caesar took his revenge, sending fifty thousand troops to attack the Eburones, a slaughter that Caesar claimed wiped out the Eburones forever.

Caesar's war in Gaul ended in 50 BCE. Historians estimate that his men killed up to one million people in the region, including women and children. In Rome, Caesar won praise for extending Rome's rule. But some leading Romans thought he had gone too far with his massacres of civilians.

Caesar, though, was not done. In 49 BCE, he marched his troops back to Rome, starting a bloody civil war that would lead to his becoming Rome's sole leader. His rule, though, didn't last. Some Roman lawmakers opposed his ruling as a dictator. On March 15, 44 BCE, a group of them attacked Caesar and stabbed him to death.

The young Caesar had been shaped by the violence all around him. Instead of turning away from it, he embraced it. Mass slaughter of foreigners and killing his own people gave him the power he craved. But in the end, he died by the same violence that had marked his life. And he set Rome on a new path—future leaders would rule as emperors, following his example of one-man rule over a growing empire.

# ATTILA THE HUN

## (CA. 406–453 CE)

A scourge is a type of whip used to punish someone. A scourge can also be the person who carries out a punishment. During the 440s, a king called Attila led his armies against the Roman Empire. He ruled the Huns. To the Romans, the Huns were one in a long line of "barbarians"—uneducated people who lived outside the empire and sometimes attacked it. The Huns, though, proved to be among the deadliest barbarians to invade Roman lands.

Attila and his men may have lacked formal education, but they were fierce, skilled warriors.

As Attila's armies destroyed cities, some Christians who survived called the Hun leader "the scourge of God." To them, God had sent Attila to punish them for their sins. Attila, though, was no Christian, and he didn't see the hand of the Christian God directing his actions. He simply wanted money and land for himself and his people.

The Huns first lived in Central Asia. They did not leave behind any books or other writings, so details about their early history are sketchy. They were nomads—people who moved from place to place to find grazing lands for their animals. The animals, in turn, provided the Huns with food and clothing, as well as horses for transportation.

By around 370, the Huns had moved west from their homeland toward the borders of the Roman Empire. They mostly lived in the Caucasus Mountains, which sit between the Black and Caspian Seas. But they raided Roman lands near the Danube River, which flows into the Black Sea in present-day Romania. Like many nomads of Central Asia, the Huns were expert horse riders. They fought on horseback, firing arrows as they rode, before moving in to finish off their enemies with swords.

Attila and his brother Bleda were Hunnish princes who started their military training at an early age. They learned to ride horses, fire arrows, and fight with swords. And while the Romans considered the Huns barbarians, the princes most likely learned the Romans' language, Latin. By the time Attila was a young man, most of the Huns had moved farther west, settling on plains that are now part of Hungary. His uncle Rua was king of the Huns, and his people's military skills sent waves of fear through the Romans. They agreed to pay Rua tribute—money that would keep the Huns from attacking.

The details of Attila's early life are not very clear. Some historians say it's impossible to know for sure how he lived and what he did. But it seems that he and his brother were destined to rule after Rua, who apparently had no sons. (Some historians, though, suggest that Rua did have sons, and Attila and Bleda had them murdered.)

Sometime around 434, Rua died and Attila and Bleda began ruling the kingdom. Several years later, the brothers demanded an increased tribute from the Romans. Wanting to avoid war, the Romans agreed, doubling the tribute to seven hundred pounds of gold every year. But Attila wanted even more wealth, and in 441 the Huns crossed the Danube River into what is now Serbia.

Over the next twelve years, the Huns pushed deeper and deeper into the Roman Empire. Tribes they had conquered, such as the Goths, joined them in the invasion. The Hun forces attacked dozens of cities as they ripped across Europe, seizing gold and silver and capturing enslaved people. Some of the precious metals went to Attila's generals, to keep their loyalty.

But Attila believed he was worthy of more than riches. One ancient historian wrote that Attila was convinced that he had been chosen by the gods of the Huns to rule the world. By the middle of the 440s, it was Attila alone who ruled the Huns. According to several accounts, he had ordered his brother killed, and at times, he had his Hunnish enemies or foreign spies impaled. While still alive, their bodies were pierced with sharpened poles, and then they were left to die.

Attila was ruthless in his quest for wealth and power. He completely destroyed some cities, leaving dead bodies to rot in the streets. Attila also ordered the killing of Christian monks. One scholar of the time wrote, "Attila ground almost the whole of Europe into dust."

A Greek diplomat named Priscus once met Attila and wrote that he was not a complete monster. Although he craved wealth, he lived simply for a king. While his guests ate off gold or silver plates, his were made of wood. Attila was loyal to his men, and he could show mercy to people who asked for it. A few Romans chose to live under his rule. They considered him a fair man who kept his word. But when at war, Attila showed no mercy to his enemies.

Attila's path of destruction continued in 451, as he made his deepest push into western Europe. The Huns got as far as Orléans, France, where a Roman army held off Attila's forces. Attila retreated to his lands in Hungary, then set out the next year to attack Italy. Once again, his men wiped out entire cities. This time, a lack of food and the spread of disease forced Attila to stop his march. The next year, he died in his palace in Hungary after celebrating his own wedding.

Attila knew the destruction he brought to Europe. He supposedly once said, "There, where I have passed, the grass will never grow again." The empire he built collapsed soon after his death. But for centuries, his name continued to strike fear in Europeans who knew of his bloodthirsty ways.

# GENGHIS KHAN
## (CA. 1162–1227)

During the twelfth century, warfare was a common part of life for the different tribes of Mongolia, in Central Asia. These nomadic tribes roamed lands that bordered China. They often battled one another, and they clashed with the Chinese as well. During this time of turmoil, a young man from one Mongol tribe emerged as a great general and political leader. His name was Temüjin, but the world remembers him today as Genghis Khan: "universal ruler." He and his sons built the largest empire ever known. Historians judge him as one of the most important figures in world history. But his path to "universal rule" was covered in the blood of tens of thousands of innocent people.

Life was hard for the nomads of Mongolia. The climate was harsh, with short summers and bitterly cold winters. Farming was almost impossible, so the tribes of the region raised herd animals, such as goats and sheep. Tribes might go to war over control of grazing land. At times, leaders from neighboring Chinese kingdoms tried to weaken the tribes by urging one to attack another.

Although the Mongols faced many struggles, Temüjin seems to have been destined to achieve great things. Legends sprang up about his birth. One said that when he was born, he held a piece of dried blood in his hand. Some Mongols believed it meant that he would become a great warrior and defeat many enemies. As his life went on, Temüjin and his soldiers seemed to make blood flow in whatever lands they conquered.

Like the other nomads of the region, the Mongols fought on horseback, and Temüjin began learning how to ride when he was only three years old.

His father led a small group of Mongols, but he died when Temüjin was nine. He should have taken his father's role as leader. But because of his age, the other men of the tribe rejected his authority. They took most of Temüjin's family's wealth, and for a time, the family survived on roots, berries, and small animals that they hunted.

As a teenager, Temüjin was captured by a Mongol tribe and held as a prisoner. He managed to escape, but he learned the importance of having allies to help protect him. He hoped to eventually command others, as his father had. Temüjin began to make friends with the leaders of other tribes and recruited soldiers to follow him. Other tribal leaders feared Temüjin's growing influence, and in 1187, a rival named Jamukha destroyed Temüjin's forces in battle. Despite that loss, Temüjin and his army defeated other Mongol tribes. The losing soldiers who refused to join Temüjin were killed. Temüjin's power grew, and in 1204, he took revenge on Jamukha, beating his army and capturing him. By one account, Temüjin then turned his enemy over to one of Jamukha's own nephews, who hated his uncle. Temüjin knew the nephew would gladly kill Jamukha, and he did, hacking him to pieces.

Two years later, all the tribes of Mongolia recognized Temüjin as their leader. He had united the tribes for the first time, earning him the title Genghis Khan. The Mongol leader's power grew as other people in Central Asia pledged their loyalty to him. One religious leader said God had told him, "I have given the whole earth to Temüjin and his sons." More Mongols came to believe this. So did Genghis. Believing that he had God's blessing, he began to attack other Central Asian empires to take their herds and weaken their militaries.

Genghis Khan's biggest target was northern China, ruled then by people called the Jurchens. He launched his major invasion in 1211, and the fighting continued for years. The typical Mongol tactic was to seize and destroy cities. At times, Genghis would kill all the residents and burn the cities to the ground, then threaten to do the same to neighboring cities if they did not surrender. By stirring fear across Central Asia, Genghis extended his rule. But when fear did not work, the Mongols were ready to fight in the most brutal ways. Genghis's men sometimes used captured enemies as human shields. One Jurchen poet wrote that after the Mongols invaded, "I only know north of the river there is no life: crumbled houses, scattered chimney smoke from a few homes."

After defeating the Jurchens and other Chinese peoples, Genghis Khan turned his attention to the west. The massacres in China were just a rehearsal for the huge slaughters to come. In Khwarazm, which included parts of what are now Afghanistan, Iran, Turkmenistan, and Uzbekistan, the Mongols once again attacked entire cities. Armies led by Genghis's sons forced the cities to surrender and killed their citizens along with their soldiers. In the city of Merv, one of the sons followed his father's order to kill everyone but not before torturing some of the wealthiest citizens to learn where they had stashed their money and valuable property.

One modern historian suggested that Genghis Khan did not order these mass killings out of cruelty but out of military necessity. His Mongol forces were often outnumbered. Genghis could not risk sparing the lives of people who might one day regain their strength and numbers and attack him. But the result was still the same: Dozens of cities destroyed, and hundreds of thousands of civilians killed.

By 1225, Genghis Khan and his armies had won control of a large part of Asia. Although Genghis's victories came from military force, he was a wise ruler. He let people worship as they pleased and promoted trade. He also rewarded people based on their talents, not whether they came from a wealthy or royal family.

In 1226, Genghis faced a rebellion from the Tanguts, people the Mongols had earlier defeated. When the Tangut commander refused to surrender, Genghis vowed to defeat the Tanguts, and he did, in what one modern historian called a bloodbath. This was his final victory. Genghis Khan died the next year.

After his death, his sons carried out his last order: to kill the ruler of the Tanguts and everyone in their capital city. They then divided up the empire their father had built and continued to expand its borders. The Mongol invasions remain infamous for their vast destruction, as Genghis sought to carry out God's prediction of his greatness. His burial site remains a mystery to this day, although it is believed to be near the sacred mountain of Burkhan Khaldun in the Khentii Province of northeastern Mongolia.

# TOMÁS DE TORQUEMADA
## (1420–1498)

Many people have the opportunity to follow any religion they choose, or none at all. But in fifteenth-century Spain, a lot of people did not have that freedom. Jewish people living in Spain at that time were forced to join the Catholic Church or face death. Many were baptized as Catholics but still secretly practiced their old faith. These Jews became targets of the Spanish Inquisition.

Under the direction of Tomás de Torquemada, thousands of Jewish people were put on trial for falsely claiming to be Catholics. Many were tortured and killed. Although the Inquisition, a period of interrogation and harsh questioning, was ordered by the king and queen of Spain and many people carried it out, Torquemada was the "Grand Inquisitor." He was the person in charge of finding out who was telling the truth about which religion they really practiced. His name is still connected to the religious terror that spread through Spain.

That country was not the first to seek out and punish people who did not strictly follow the teachings of the Catholic Church. Starting in the twelfth century, Catholic kings and religious leaders in other parts of Europe went after heretics— people who chose not to follow some of their Catholic beliefs. The accused heretics faced trials called inquests. That is the source of the word *inquisition*—a legal panel established to question people about their faith. At first, people judged to be heretics were simply kicked out of the church. But over time, heretics faced other punishments. They could be sent to prison, have their land taken away, or be tortured. The torture was used to force the accused to confess to their religious crimes (that they were not, in fact, practicing the Catholic faith). Those who didn't confess were tied to a wooden stake and burned.

While earlier inquisitions focused on Christian heretics, the Spanish Inquisition was particularly focused on Jews. Starting in the eighth century, Islamic armies conquered most of Spain. The Muslim leaders allowed Jewish people to freely practice their religion. But by the 1480s, when Queen Isabella I and King Ferdinand II ruled most of Spain, the country was once again Catholic. Spanish Jews were pressured to convert.

The man chosen to lead the Spanish Inquisition was already well known to Queen Isabella I. Torquemada came from a strong religious background. One of his uncles, Juan de Torquemada, was a cardinal—a high-ranking priest—in the Catholic Church. (In Catholicism, only the pope, the head of the church, has more power than a cardinal.) Even though his family had been Jewish, the uncle deeply embraced his faith, like Torquemada did later on. Their family had converted decades before Torquemada was born. Some converts seek to prove their devotion to their new faith by strictly following its teachings. That became true with Torquemada.

Like his uncle, Torquemada belonged to a Roman Catholic order called the Dominicans. Many members became great scholars, as Torquemada did. They were also expected to live a simple life and avoid owning many possessions. Torquemada took this seriously. He never wore clothes made of linen, a soft cloth, and he didn't eat meat.

Thanks to his religious devotion, Torquemada was put in charge of a convent, the home of nuns. At one point, he met young Isabella, the future queen of Spain. Torquemada heard her confessions, the Catholic practice of asking for forgiveness for sins. After Isabella married King Ferdinand II and became queen, Torquemada served as a political adviser to both royal rulers.

Dominican priests were tasked with finding and punishing heretics wherever they found them. Because of this, they became the favorite inquisitors of the popes. Torquemada took that duty seriously, carrying it to bloody ends for Spain's Jewish population. In 1482, Torquemada was named an assistant inquisitor. The next year, the pope made him the Grand Inquisitor in Spain.

Torquemada fully embraced his role as the hunter of heretics. He wrote down the rules describing how to carry out inquisitions for panels of judges who asked all the questions. That included the use of torture to make Jewish people confess they were still practicing Judaism. Torquemada also encouraged Catholics to watch for signs that their neighbors might secretly be Jews. One suspicious activity was not eating pork, which is a Jewish dietary law.

Some of the accused heretics were tied to a wooden rack and painfully stretched. Those who confessed to being heretics were then whipped in public.

The ones who did not confess were marched through their towns and then tied to wooden stakes surrounded by piles of firewood. Before the flame was lit, monks and priests gave the accused person one more chance to confess to their crimes. If they did, they were spared a fiery death: They were strangled instead. If not, they were burned at the stake.

Historians aren't sure how many died during the Spanish Inquisition under Torquemada's orders.

Some sources say two to three thousand people were burned alive, while many more were strangled. Some also escaped death, but they were enslaved or returned to prison, where they faced even more torture.

In addition to rooting out all Jews who claimed to be practicing the Catholic faith, Torquemada also wanted Jews who had not become Catholic to be expelled from, or forced out of, Spain. In 1492, Queen Isabella I and King Ferdinand II followed his advice. All Jewish people in the country or lands controlled by Spain had to leave their homes behind and move on. Many settled in North Africa, Italy, and Turkey. Some other religious leaders opposed the power Torquemada had won for himself as Grand Inquisitor. In 1494, Pope Alexander VI, the head of the Catholic Church, forced Torquemada to share his power with other inquisitors. He began to lose his influence over the way the Inquisition was carried out. Two years later, he retired to a monastery (a place where monks live) in Ávila, Spain. Torquemada died there in 1498. But the Inquisition continued for several centuries longer.

Torquemada had done what he believed his

Catholic faith required him to do—destroy those who would not willingly accept it. He made his deadly mark, with the torture and murder of everyone he deemed to be a heretic. It is rumored that after his tomb was robbed in the 1830s, Torquemada's bones were burned as a public punishment and reminder of all those he had tortured during his own lifetime.

# VLAD THE IMPALER
## (CA. 1431–CA. 1477)

Dracula, history's most famous vampire, was the product of the imagination of the author Bram Stoker. But the name for his creation has roots in real life. In Romanian, *dracul* means "dragon." A fifteenth-century prince from a part of Romania called Wallachia was known as Vlad II Dracul. His son was called Vlad III Dracula—Vlad, son of the dragon. Stoker came across that name while doing research for his book. The real Dracula was no vampire, but he was famous for his bloody ways. His cruelty earned him the Romanian nickname Vlad Țepeș—Vlad the Impaler.

His father, Vlad II Dracul, belonged to a group of princes known in English as the Order of the Dragon. Members of the order were expected to defend the Christian lands of Europe from invading Muslim forces. Christians and Muslims had been battling each other for centuries. By the time Vlad ruled, the biggest threat came from the Muslim Ottoman Empire, centered in what is now Turkey.

Young Vlad got caught up in the politics of the day when he was eleven or twelve. His father wanted to create a better relationship with the Turks of the Ottoman Empire. He agreed to turn over Vlad and another son to the Turks. As long as the Turks held the boys, Vlad II Dracul was not likely to oppose the Ottoman Empire. Young Vlad left no record of how it felt to be taken from his family and held as a hostage for about six years. Modern historians, though, wonder if it shaped his later bloody deeds.

By some accounts, Vlad and his brother were treated well. The Turks educated the boys, and they learned to speak Turkish. But Vlad was not always a polite guest. He could be violent, and it was said even his guards were at times scared of him.

Although Vlad avoided harsh treatment, his time as a prisoner in Turkey stoked his hatred of his captors. He also learned that terrorizing people with extreme violence would gain their obedience.

The Turks released Vlad and his brother in 1448. Vlad returned to Wallachia and learned his father and another brother had been killed by local nobles who opposed Vlad II Dracul's rule. Young Vlad ruled briefly in 1448, thanks to the support of the Turks, but another Wallachian prince forced him from power. By 1456, the political situation had changed: Vlad's rival prince was allied with the Turks, who were trying to seize lands in the area. With the backing of some Hungarians, who were Christian, Vlad returned to power in Wallachia. This time, he ruled for six years. During that time, he committed the terrible acts that led to his vivid nickname, Vlad the Impaler.

Forgetting for a time about the threat of the Turks to Eastern Europe, Vlad focused on strengthening his rule in Wallachia. That meant getting rid of his local enemies. They included the nobles that Vlad suspected had killed his father and brother. Vlad laid a trap for them. He invited them to a feast, then had his soldiers arrest them. Vlad forced the nobles to march into the mountains and build him a castle! The men who survived the difficult work were then impaled: Vlad ordered that a large pole with one sharpened end be driven through the men's bodies while they were still alive. The poles were then stuck in the ground, and Vlad watched the men die slow, painful deaths.

Nobles weren't the only local citizens who faced Vlad's anger. He wanted everyone he ruled to work, and he did not like to see beggars, even if they were sick or physically disabled. By one account, he invited many of the poor and sick people of Wallachia to another feast, then locked them in the hall and set it on fire. No one escaped. Another time, Vlad saw a man wearing a shirt with sleeves that weren't long enough to cover his arms. The prince had the man's wife impaled because, in Vlad's mind, she should have made sure her husband had a shirt with long sleeves.

Along with impaling or burning his victims, Vlad found other drastic ways to enforce his style of law and order. One source from 1488 described how he roasted three people alive and forced others to eat them. If wives were not faithful to their husbands, Vlad had the women skinned alive. When two diplomats visited him, they took off their hats but not the caps they wore underneath. Vlad asked them to remove the caps as well, but the diplomats said it was their custom to keep them on. The insulted prince made sure the caps would stay on—he had them nailed into the diplomats' heads.

Vlad carried out perhaps the largest mass impaling in 1462. While battling an invading Turkish army, he launched a night raid on his enemy's camp and captured twenty thousand prisoners, including women and children. Vlad then took the prisoners to his capital city in Wallachia. When the Turks advanced on the city, they found the bodies of the prisoners, who had been impaled on poles lining the road. Vlad wanted to scare his enemy, and it worked. The Turks retreated.

During his six-year rule, Vlad killed as many as one hundred thousand men, women, and children in his land. He did not spare fellow Christians and even ordered the slaughter of Germans living in Wallachia.

Vlad burned their entire village to the ground.

Most of the accounts of Vlad's atrocities were written after his death. Historians warn that some of the stories may not be true. The printing press was still a new invention, and printers sometimes filled their works with horror to attract readers. And some of the stories were written by Turks or Germans. Since they were often his victims, they believed Vlad was a monster, even if he didn't commit all the horrible murders they claimed he did. But one account of his terrible acts came from Vlad himself, in a letter he wrote in 1462 while battling the Turks: "I have killed peasants, men and women, old and young. . . . We killed 23,884 Turks without counting those whom we burned in homes or the Turks whose heads were not cut by our soldiers."

Vlad and the Turks remained enemies through the rest of his life. In 1477, Turkish troops caught Vlad and his men by surprise, and Vlad met his own gruesome end. After the Turks killed him, they cut off his head and sent it to the ruler of the Ottoman Empire. The soldiers wanted to prove that they had killed the man who had murdered so many Turks.

Stories of Vlad's cruelty spread throughout German territories and Russia. Books about his techniques of torture and punishments became best sellers. Centuries later, Vlad III Dracula's bloody biography became a part of the story of the famous vampire who carried his name.

# HERNÁN CORTÉS
## (1485–1547)

Beginning in 1492, Christopher Columbus made four separate voyages to the Americas for the king and queen of Spain. With each, more European monarchs began to understand the value of the lands to the west that were previously unknown to them. Spain's King Ferdinand II and Queen Isabella I had two goals: They wanted to bring gold and other valuable resources from the Americas back to Spain. And they wanted to spread their Roman Catholic faith in the lands they now claimed as their own. One of the soldiers who led this effort to seize colonies for Spain was Hernán Cortés.

Cortés and the men he commanded were called conquistadors, a word that means *conqueror*. These men were sent to the Caribbean and Central and South America to explore there and take control of the people they met by any means necessary. They wanted to seize the land and the mineral wealth they found there—like gold and silver—for the king and queen. For Cortés, that meant massacring native populations, killing thousands of warriors and civilians.

The Spanish conquistadors came from different backgrounds. Some had wealthy families, but others did not. In Spain, they might have been artisans or traders, soldiers or sailors. But even those who had not served in the military had some training as fighters.

Cortés's parents had both come from old, honorable families, but by the time Cortés was born, they had little money. Young Cortés showed great intelligence, but he also had a quick temper. When he was fourteen, his parents sent him away to school, hoping he would one day become a lawyer. But he had other ideas. When Cortés was just a boy, Christopher Columbus had claimed land in the Americas for Spain.

A new age of exploration was beginning, and Cortés wanted to be part of it.

Cortés decided to become a soldier and serve his country in the Americas. In 1504, he sailed to the island of Hispaniola, which today is divided into two countries: Haiti and the Dominican Republic. The island was one of the first in the Caribbean Sea that Spain controlled. Cortés made clear why he came to the Caribbean region: He, like the Spanish king, wanted gold. But Cortés was also religious, and he wanted to spread the Catholic faith as well.

After spending several years on Hispaniola, Cortés moved on to the island of Cuba. There, he heard from other Spanish explorers about the riches of Mexico. Most of the country was under the rule of the Aztec nation, who had built their own empire and ruled several hundred smaller states that they had conquered. The people they had defeated in these surrounding states sent gold and other valuables in tribute to the Aztec ruler, Montezuma II.

In 1519, Cortés and about five hundred soldiers sailed from Cuba to the east coast of Mexico. He was determined to find, and take, the Aztecs' riches.

To make sure his men could not desert him on the inland journey, he ordered most of his ships destroyed at the water's edge. He said that he and his men "would conquer and win the land or die in the attempt."

Cortés and his troops then began to work their way from the coast into the heart of the country. Along the way, the Spanish battled some of the native people who lived there. Others, though, agreed to join Cortés's expedition. They didn't like being ruled by the Aztecs, and they saw that the Europeans had powerful weapons and large animals they had never seen before—horses. These smaller tribal nations thought Cortés and his men could help them win their freedom from the Aztecs.

On the march westward toward the Aztec capital of Tenochtitlán, Cortés and his men carried out a massacre in the city of Cholula. Some historians say that Cortés believed that the people of Cholula planned to carry out a sneak attack against him. And so, Cortés decided to strike first. He managed to have several thousand unarmed Cholulan warriors gathered into the city square. Then the Spaniards and their native allies killed the defenseless men.

As many as six thousand Cholulans died in just a few hours (though some sources say the killings went on for several days).

By November 1519, Cortés and his men had reached Tenochtitlán. At first, Cortés and Montezuma II seemed to have established a good relationship. But after Cortés kidnapped the Aztec leader, war seemed to be the only outcome. Fighting erupted in June 1520, and the Aztecs drove the Spaniards from the city.

Cortés and his men then began to prepare for a final assault on Tenochtitlán. More Spanish troops arrived from Spain and the Caribbean islands under Spanish rule. Cortés and his local allies built boats that could bring troops across the lake that surrounded Tenochtitlán. And Cortés and his men carried out raids against surrounding villages. In most cases, the people surrendered, rather than fight the Spanish.

By the end of 1520, Cortés was ready to attack Tenochtitlán again. His army now included tens of thousands of native allies. First, though, early in 1521, he ordered an attack on the village of Tecoaque. The people there were allied with the Aztecs and had earlier attacked Spanish soldiers traveling through the region. Cortés's men killed women and children in Tecoaque and destroyed the temples.

Cortés then turned his attention back to Tenochtitlán. With his new, larger army, he began a siege of the city in May 1521. The goal of a siege is to cut off supplies to the enemy trapped in a city. Over time, they would become too weak to defend themselves or be forced to surrender.

At Tenochtitlán, the Spanish first cut off the supply of fresh water to the city. Fighting began soon after. When the Spanish entered the city, they destroyed bridges and buildings. Starvation—along with the diseases the Spaniards had brought to Mexico— killed thousands of Aztec people. The fighting itself killed as many as one hundred thousand Aztecs living within Tenochtitlán. In August, the Aztecs surrendered. Cortés had carried out his promise to conquer Mexico.

After his military victory, Cortés began to pursue his other major goal—to wipe out the Aztec religion. His men destroyed temples and sometimes built Catholic churches on the same sites. Cortés distributed the occupied land to his men, and the local people were required to work for their new Spanish masters.

For a time, Cortés was the governor of New Spain, the name the Spanish gave these new colonies. He also continued to explore, reaching as far west as what is now Baja California. Cortés returned to Spain in 1541. Although he had become wealthy, he felt the Spanish government did not respect all he had done for the country. Cortés died in Spain in 1547. He is still considered to be one of the most brutal conquistadors. Today in Mexico, some people consider him one of history's greatest villains. They have asked Spain to apologize for the slaughter he carried out in the name of the Spanish king. So far, Spain has refused to apologize for the conquistador who destroyed the Aztec empire.

# QUEEN MARY I OF ENGLAND
## (1516–1558)

During the sixteenth century, England was ruled by a royal family named the Tudors. The family was divided over religion, and their country was as well. Personal desires and differing faiths led to decades of turmoil. For five years, Mary Tudor ruled as England's queen. She came to be known as "Bloody Mary."

England's battle over religion began with Mary's father, King Henry VIII. He considered himself a good Catholic until church teachings got in the way of his love for a young woman named Anne Boleyn. Henry was already married to Catherine of Aragon, and the Catholic Church did not believe in divorce. Henry was desperate to marry Anne, hoping she could do what Catherine had failed to do—give birth to a son who would one day be king. Catherine and Henry had only been able to produce one child: their daughter, Mary.

Catherine was a devout Catholic, and she raised Mary in the Catholic faith. The young princess also received a good education—one worthy of a queen. (Since Mary would one day rule England if Henry never had a son.) Catherine was the daughter of the king and queen of Spain, and Mary had warm feelings for her mother's homeland. When Mary was still a child, Henry thought of marrying his daughter to King Charles V of Spain. It was common for European rulers of the day to arrange marriages between their children at a young age. Charles, though, ended up marrying a princess from Portugal.

Henry treated his daughter well—until he realized that he could not divorce Catherine so he could marry Anne Boleyn. Although he was still married to Catherine, he refused to accept her as his wife. Then Henry said Mary could no longer see her mother. This devastated the girl, since she was so close to Catherine.

In 1533, Henry married Anne Boleyn, even though the Catholic Church refused to end his marriage to Catherine. Henry created a new church, which he called the Church of England. Under his church's laws, Henry had the right to marry Anne because his marriage to Catherine had not been a legal marriage. During the rest of Henry's life and for several years after, the Church of England overturned Catholic teachings and drew close to Protestant beliefs. Those included putting the teachings of the Bible at the center of the faith, not the words of priests and other religious leaders. (Protestants are members of the Christian faith who do not recognize the pope as the leader of the church.)

Mary saw her own status lowered after Henry divorced her mother. She lost her title of princess and at times feared Henry's second wife, Anne Boleyn, might order that she be killed. Mary refused to recognize Henry's divorce and his new marriage. Meanwhile, Catherine was treated like a prisoner, and she and Mary never saw each other again.

Henry said he would forgive Mary if she acknowledged he was the head of the new Church of England. Mary, still a devout Catholic, refused.

For several decades, Mary watched first her father and then her half brother, Edward, weaken the Catholic Church in England. That included closing monasteries. Many of the monasteries had amassed great wealth through the contributions and donations of the Catholic people, which Henry wanted for himself. When some Catholic leaders resisted the closings, Henry had them hanged. Under Edward, some Catholics rebelled against the introduction of Protestant teachings. They were quickly killed.

Henry died in 1547, and Edward VI became king. After her half brother died in 1553, Mary became queen at last. Mary had a unique position—she was the first woman to serve as England's queen without being married to a king. She was determined to use her power to overturn the religious changes made by Henry and Edward. Mary wanted England to be a Catholic country again. Some Protestants feared for their lives, knowing Mary could charge them with being heretics (those who didn't believe in the

Catholic faith). They fled the country rather than face trial. If they were convicted of being heretics, they could be burned at the stake. (Protestant rulers had earlier done the same to Catholics.)

But not all Protestants fled, and about 280 died fiery deaths at the stake. The executions were public events, with average citizens turning out to watch. At one burning, two guilty Protestant ministers were first chained to a wooden stake. Piles of wood that reached as high as their necks surrounded them. The men also had bags of gunpowder tied around their necks. (This was considered a sign of mercy! The exploding powder would kill the men faster than the flames would.)

Bartholomew Traheron, one English Protestant who did flee his homeland, heard reports of Mary's killings. He wrote that the queen was swimming "in the holy blood of most innocent, virtuous, and excellent personages."

Mary, like other rulers of the day, also executed people she considered political traitors. She faced a rebellion in 1554 when she announced her plan to marry Prince Philip II of Spain. Philip was Catholic, and some English feared he hoped to one day rule England himself. Several thousand rebels led by Sir Thomas Wyatt marched on London, but Mary's army ended the uprising. Rather than having him face the heretics' punishment of death by flame, Mary made sure that Wyatt's head was chopped off—the punishment for treason, or trying to betray one's country. His head, along with his severed limbs, was put on public display. The body parts were a gruesome reminder of what happened to traitors.

Mary died of an illness in 1558, at the age of forty-two, paving the way for her half sister, Elizabeth, to take the throne. Under Elizabeth I, England became Protestant once again—and the killing continued. Some Catholics were now burned as heretics; others were executed as traitors.

During the years of Elizabeth I's reign, Protestants began to build up the deadly reputation of "Bloody Mary." Because of her efforts to restore Catholicism in England, they wanted to be sure her legacy was presented in the most negative way. And those ideas about Mary have lasted a very long time. But some historians now suggest that Mary doesn't quite deserve her nickname. They point out that her sister and father were responsible for far more deaths. And her reputation was created by men who resented her as queen. Even so, for the short time she ruled, Mary made her Protestant subjects fear for their lives.

# IVAN THE TERRIBLE
## (1530–1584)

Creating a new nation with a strong government is no easy task. But Ivan IV of Moscow was determined to do it. Moscow is the capital of Russia today, a sprawling nation that covers more land than any other country except Canada. But in Ivan's day, Moscow was just one of several independent states. Some were called principalities, because they were ruled by princes. To create a new Russian nation, Ivan had to lead his armies against European principalities to his west and the remains of the Mongol empire to his east. He also had to weaken the power of Moscow's boyars.

These men were the most important princes and landowners of his realm. Ivan used violence and terror to help him achieve his goals. Today, we know him as Ivan the Terrible.

The process of expanding Moscow's power had begun decades before. Under Ivan's grandfather, Ivan III, Moscow won its independence from the Mongols. They had dominated Central Asia since the rampages of Genghis Khan and his sons during the thirteenth century. Then, the earlier Ivan began forcing other Russian princes to accept his rule over them. Some princes willingly agreed to serve him rather than face a battle.

Ivan III's son, Vasily III, ruled Moscow next. He died in 1533, making his son, Ivan IV, the new grand prince of Moscow. Since the boy was only three years old, his mother, Yelena, ruled Moscow until Ivan was eight. Then Moscow's boyars competed to rule the principality. Ivan saw the chaos that came when Moscow lacked a single strong leader. He also grew to distrust the boyars.

A powerful boyar named Ivan Shuisky first upset the boy when he had Ivan's caretaker arrested and carried away in chains. Shuisky wanted to control who would have influence over Ivan. Over the next several years, Ivan later claimed, Shuisky and others denied him food and clean clothes. Ivan wrote in a letter years later that he received "no human care from any quarter." Some modern historians think that the way the boyars treated Ivan stirred his later violence against them.

At age sixteen, Ivan finally took control of Moscow. To show that his power was absolute, Ivan gave himself the title "tsar of all Russia." The word *tsar* comes from the Latin word *caesar*, or "emperor." Ivan was trying to make a connection between his rule and the emperors of ancient Rome. Like other Christian rulers of the day, Ivan also claimed that his right to rule came from God.

Weakening the power of the boyars was among Ivan's first goals. He had already shown a taste of what he thought of them. In 1546, he executed three boyars in front of the troops he commanded. A modern historian wrote that Ivan did it to entertain his soldiers. Shortly after becoming tsar, he had one boyar's son impaled. While attacking the boyars,

Ivan sought the loyalty of a different groups of men by giving them newly taken lands.

Ivan didn't waste any time in engaging his foreign enemies, either. Soon after taking power, he turned his armies against the people called Tatars. They lived along the Volga River in Kazan. Ivan attacked them several times before carrying out a successful siege of their capital in 1552. His men slaughtered the city's defeated soldiers, took women and children as prisoners, and carried off all the valuables they could find. Ivan's success against the Tatars led to his Russian nickname, *grozny*. It means "inspiring awe," but at some point, the English translation became "terrible," giving Ivan the name he's best known by today.

Ivan then looked toward Europe, and in 1558, his forces attacked Livonia, in what is now Latvia and Estonia. The war dragged on. The Livonians received aid from Poland and Sweden. When the fighting ended, Russia had lost all the land it had gained earlier in the war.

During the war against Livonia and its allies, Ivan's hatred of the boyars grew even more. In 1565, he claimed that some, along with church officials, were traitors. His anger might have also been fueled by the recent death of his wife Anastasiya. Together, they had six children, though only two, both boys, survived childhood. One historian believes that Anastasiya had helped control Ivan's bouts of anger and suspicion of others. With her gone, his true character returned even stronger than before.

Ivan's battles were now both on foreign soil and at home. He created his own private police force, called the *oprichniki*. Dressed in black, the *oprichniki* terrorized the boyars and other wealthy Russians. The *oprichniki* were said to carry a broom, to suggest they were sweeping away Ivan's enemies. Some sources said they also tied dogs' heads to their horses, a sign that they were nipping at the boyars' heels or coming after them like a pack of dogs.

Under Ivan's command, the *oprichniki* forced the boyars off their lands. Some nobles fled, while others were executed, along with the people who worked for them. In 1570, Ivan led the *oprichniki* against the city of Novgorod. With the attack on his own people in Novgorod, Ivan and his men destroyed buildings and food supplies. About two thousand citizens were executed, though many more died of starvation. The dead included many women and children.

In 1572, Ivan ended the *oprichniki*, but his foreign wars continued. So did his quarrels with the boyars. He still wanted to assert his power as the ruler of Russia. Ivan even turned his anger against one of his own sons, who was also named Ivan. In 1581, the tsar argued with his son over who should lead an army against Polish forces attacking Russia. Ivan the Terrible struck his son in the head with a long stick. The younger Ivan died several days later.

After killing his son, Ivan the Terrible ruled Russia for three more years, until his own death in 1584. He died away from the battlefield, while playing a game of chess. Fyodor, the last surviving son from his marriage to Anastasiya, then became the tsar. (Ivan had had several other marriages after Anastasiya's death.)

Ivan did not conquer all the foreign lands he sought. But he did weaken the power of the Russian princes. He carried out enough bloody violence to ensure that he would be remembered as "the terrible."

# ELIZABETH BÁTHORY
## (1560–1614)

The legend began in the late eighteenth century, almost two hundred years after Elizabeth Báthory took her last breath. While she was alive, this rich and powerful Hungarian countess learned that she could keep her skin looking young forever. Her beauty secret? Bathing in the blood of girls and young women.

Elizabeth Báthory was said to have discovered the blood's powers by accident. One day she struck a young female servant, causing blood to spurt from the girl's nose and onto Báthory. The countess then noticed that her skin seemed smoother where the blood had landed. From then on, to get all the blood she needed to remain youthful, Elizabeth began killing hundreds of girls. Rumors of the countess's bloody beauty ritual spread, until the story made its way into a book in 1796.

There's only one problem with this ghoulish legend—it is simply a legend and not historically true. But a part of the story is based in fact: Elizabeth Báthory did kill young women, sometimes after torturing them. Today, she is remembered as the "Blood Countess."

When Elizabeth was born, her family owned estates in Transylvania, in what is now Romania. At the time, the region was part of Hungary. Her uncle Stephen was the prince of Transylvania and later was named the king of Poland.

Elizabeth grew up in a castle, surrounded by great wealth. She was also surrounded by relatives who may have had some dark secrets. One of her aunts and an uncle were rumored to have influenced Elizabeth with some dangerous—and even satanic—ideas.

When she was a teenager, Elizabeth married

a Hungarian military hero from another wealthy family. The couple moved into a castle in Čachtice, in what is now Slovakia. For a time, Elizabeth seemed like any other wealthy woman of her era. She raised four children and oversaw the servants who took care of the family castle.

But inside the castle, horrible things were taking place. Among the servants working there were young peasant girls from surrounding villages. Relatives of the girls sometimes reported that they never returned to their families' homes. Rumors spread that Elizabeth Báthory was torturing and then killing the girls. Local officials, however, ignored the stories. Outside of their families, no one seemed too concerned about why the girls had gone missing.

But when wealthier families began reporting that their daughters had gone missing, too, the local officials took more of an interest. In 1609, Elizabeth had invited several dozen of these young women to stay at her castle. Their parents were proud to see the countess taking an interest in them. But then the parents realized that their daughters, like the peasant girls before them, were disappearing. Elizabeth tried to explain away the reports that something evil was going on in the castle. She made the outrageous statement that some girls had murdered several other girls, then took their own lives! But she couldn't produce any evidence to support her claim.

News of the alleged murders spread through the countryside. And proof of her cruelty came to light when villagers found the bodies of four dead girls who had been tossed over the castle walls.

In 1610, news of what was happening at Báthory's castle reached the king of Hungary. He ordered a government official named György Thurzó to investigate. Thurzó was a cousin of the countess's by marriage. When he reached the castle in December, he found proof of Elizabeth Báthory's cruelty and madness. Thurzó saw the battered body of a girl who had just been married. Searching the grounds, he found the bodies of two more girls and the rotting corpses of several others.

Thurzó arrested Báthory and four of her servants. Held separately from the countess, the servants described how she had ordered them to torture and kill the young girls who came to the castle. When a trial began in January 1611, the servants gave details of what they had seen and been ordered to do. Some of the torture was so severe that Báthory's own clothes would be covered in blood.

The servants revealed that Elizabeth Báthory's husband had taken part in the torture, too. He had died several years before, but while he was alive, he had shown his wife some of the ways to inflict pain on the innocent young girls. One method: If a girl passed out because of her beatings, she could be revived by putting lit paper between her toes.

During two trials, witnesses who had worked for Báthory described seeing dozens of brutal killings. By one account, the countess kept a book with the names of all her victims—650 of them.

Three of the countess's servants were executed for their roles in helping her. Elizabeth Báthory, though, escaped death. If she had been executed, the government could have taken all she owned. Thurzó arranged for her to be sentenced to life in prison instead, so the Báthory family could keep her land and her wealth. Báthory was placed in a room in her castle with the windows bricked up and the door sealed.

Only two small openings let her get fresh air and food. The countess died in this prison in 1614, at age fifty-four.

Since her death, the legends around the Blood Countess have grown. Some people claim that she, not Vlad the Impaler, inspired Bram Stoker to create *Dracula*. But most people who have studied Stoker's work say this isn't true. Beyond the myths, the truth of Elizabeth Báthory's cruelty is horrible enough.

# MAXIMILIEN ROBESPIERRE
## (1758–1794)

Can the fight for liberty lead to terror and mass murder? During the 1790s in France, it did. French farmers, shopkeepers, and others without much money or power wanted to have a role in their government. In 1789, the French people rose up against King Louis XVI and the rich landowners and Catholic priests who supported him. The rebels formed a new government body to create laws. This National Assembly granted French citizens free speech and freedom of religion for the first time.

But the fight for more rights and equality

turned violent. Starting in 1793, France experienced what is called the Reign of Terror. And leading the Reign of Terror was Maximilien Robespierre.

Before the revolution, Robespierre had been a lawyer, like his father. Robespierre had studied in Paris, though in the political world of the French capital, he was largely unknown. But anyone who heard him speak was impressed with his deep passion about the issues he believed in. He felt that only people of good character should run the government, and they should encourage good behavior in others as well. He came to believe that he was one of those good people and that he was entitled to use fear and panic to create a new French government.

In 1789, Robespierre was elected to the Estates-General. In theory, this branch of the French government could pass laws. But in reality, the king and his advisers directed what laws were passed. The Estates-General had three parts: one to represent France's nobles, one to represent the priests, and one to represent everyone else. Robespierre was a member of this Third Estate that represented everyone else, and its members formed the new National Assembly.

The National Assembly wanted a new government that would protect the interests of everyone, not just the rich and powerful. That meant taking away some of the king's powers and putting them in the hands of their citizens, who would elect the members of the National Assembly. Robespierre supported these efforts, and he often spoke against the king and for this new democratic government. As the revolution went on, Robespierre believed the king should be arrested and tried for treason. The lawmaker and others like him got their wish in 1792. King Louis XVI was arrested, and the National Assembly became the sole source of power in the French government. Early the next year, Louis was executed.

By then, the French revolutionaries were arguing with one another over how France should be governed. At the time, the country was also at war with several European kingdoms. The rest of Europe didn't want to see rebellion and the urge for democracy spread beyond France. Within France, some people opposed the revolution that had just taken place within their own country.

Facing all these problems, the National Assembly created the Committee of Public Safety. Its members would run the government during these difficult times. The committee included men from the two major groups of revolutionaries—the Jacobins and the Girondins. Robespierre was a Jacobin, and he was not pleased with the course of the revolution. Things were moving too slowly, he thought. He wanted the Committee of Public Safety to take bold steps to weaken the remaining power of the nobles and the Catholic Church. Robespierre believed wholeheartedly in the goals of the revolution. His passion and his great speaking skills won others to his side. He emerged as the leader of the committee during the summer of 1793.

Even before then, one of the new government's tools of terror had been put in place. Anyone labeled an "enemy of the republic" would be tried for treason. For Robespierre, enemies were anyone who didn't support his vision for the future of France. Those who were found guilty faced the guillotine. This machine of death quickly sliced off the head of anyone positioned beneath its sharp blade.

Under Robespierre, the hunt for enemies gathered steam. The Reign of Terror began in the fall of 1793. For Robespierre's Jacobins, the enemies included fellow revolutionaries—the Girondins—as well as counterrevolutionaries—the people who openly opposed the revolution. The Jacobins killed thousands of counterrevolutionaries in different parts of the country. Many were shot, while others were drowned. In Paris, up to three thousand people were killed under the guillotine, while thousands more sat in prison.

To Robespierre, this violence against the French people was for a good cause. He said the people who opposed the revolution were not citizens but "only strangers, or rather, enemies." By trying to weaken the revolution, he said, they were aiding the foreign countries that were at war with France.

In 1794, France was doing better in the battle against outside kingdoms. But Robespierre was convinced that the terror should go on. Some Jacobins, though, were tired of the killings. Others feared Robespierre would come after them next. Many believed he was acting like the tyrants he often criticized.

In July, some politicians who opposed Robespierre accused him of now being an enemy of the republic. It now was *his* turn to face the guillotine.

As France's foreign wars continued, the country struggled to keep the goals of its revolution alive. But the Jacobin leader Robespierre had a lasting influence. In seeing enemies everywhere and killing many of them, he created fear. He felt that out of fear, people would obey whoever was in charge. The Reign of Terror was a model that many later dictators followed.

# QUEEN RANAVALONA I OF MADAGASCAR
## (1778–1861)

The island of Madagascar sits in the Indian Ocean, some 250 miles off the eastern coast of Africa. Today, it is perhaps best known as the home to thousands of plant and animal species found nowhere else on Earth. But Madagascar was also once the home to one of the deadliest hearts of the nineteenth century. Queen Ranavalona I ordered the killings of thousands of people, both local residents and foreigners. Thousands more died because of her policies. Her murderous ways earned her the nickname "Ranavalona the Cruel."

Madagascar was broken up into several small kingdoms until the start of the nineteenth century. During the 1810s and 1820s, King Radama I finished the job his father had begun of uniting them. Radama sought help from both France and Great Britain to ensure his rule. He looked to Europe for ideas on how to govern. Under Radama, Madagascar created a modern military and ended its slave trade with foreign nations. He also welcomed Christian missionaries to the island. Their main job was to convince the Malagasy, the local people, to give up their traditional religion and become Christians. Radama also directed the missionaries to build schools. They also created the island's first written language.

Radama himself didn't become a Christian. By staying true to the island's traditional religions, he was able to have many wives. Ranavalona was one of twelve wives he had at the time of his death in 1828. Their families had arranged the marriage when Ranavalona was twenty-two and Radama was sixteen. The arrangement was a reward to Ranavalona's father, as he had uncovered and reported a plot to kill the king. Young Ranavalona was then adopted by the king and lived in the same royal household as her future husband.

Ranavalona was not considered Radama's favorite wife, and unlike several of the others, she never had any children with him. Some historians say King Radama I died of natural causes. Others, though, suggest that Ranavalona had her husband poisoned. With the help of two military officers, Ranavalona won enough support to have herself named Madagascar's new ruler. Then she ordered the execution of Radama's nephew, his mother, and anyone else who opposed her rule.

Ranavalona's supporters included wealthy islanders who had disliked Radama's policy of letting Christian missionaries settle in Madagascar. Like them, Ranavalona still practiced the traditional religions, and she rejected the idea of letting the British and French trade with the kingdom. She forced most of the foreign business owners to leave the island. The French responded by attacking, but many of their soldiers got sick from malaria. Ranavalona's forces defeated the French, and the queen cut off the heads of twenty-one French soldiers. She then stuck the severed heads on poles placed along the shore, as a warning to anyone else who thought about attacking Madagascar.

Ranavalona also forced the Christian missionaries to leave Madagascar. Then she began a reign of terror against Malagasy who had accepted the foreign religion. Practicing Christianity became a crime, and the local Christians had to give up their new faith. If they refused, Ranavalona had them tortured or killed. Some Christians were burned alive. Others were hung by ropes over rocky cliffs. The ropes were then cut, plunging the Christians to their deaths. People on the island called this period "the years of darkness." Along with outlawing Christianity, Ranavalona allowed some Malagasy to be enslaved and sold abroad.

Even the Malagasy who had not embraced Christianity faced Ranavalona's cruelty. Poor people who could not pay their taxes were forced to work for the government without pay. They had some freedom—for example, they could return to their own homes, though they sometimes had to walk long distances to get there. But while they worked for the queen, they were essentially enslaved. Many died from lack of food.

In 1845, the queen ordered the island's nobles to go with her on a buffalo hunt. Fifty thousand people, including soldiers and enslaved people, followed the queen through the countryside. Since the region lacked roads, Ranavalona ordered one built ahead of her as she traveled. Workers cut trees, moved rocks, and dug ditches. They also built a new town in the wilderness. Enslaved laborers worked hard, often without enough food to eat. Starvation and brutal working conditions left a string of dead bodies along the queen's new road. By one account, ten thousand people died during the "hunt," which lasted sixteen weeks. There is no record that Ranavalona ever killed a buffalo.

Along with making enemies of Christians and foreigners, Ranavalona saw her son, Rakoto, who had been born several months after Radama died, turn against her. (Most people believed Radama was not Rakoto's father.) Rakoto opposed his mother's policies and took part in at least one attempt to force her to give up the throne. His violent efforts failed, and Ranavalona executed the people who helped Rakoto. She did, however, spare her son's life.

During Ranavalona's reign, many Malagasy died in the name of law and order. If the queen suspected someone was disloyal, they faced a form of trial by ordeal (a series of dangerous tests). Under this system, a person ate three pieces of chicken. Then they were given a poison that came from a local nut, the tangena. If they vomited the poison and the chicken, the person was declared innocent. If they died from the poison, Ranavalona believed they had been guilty.

Ranavalona ruled for thirty-three years, until her death in 1861. Rakoto became King Radama II, and he once again sought good relations with European nations. But he could not erase what his mother had done.

No one knows for sure how many people died because of Ranavalona the Cruel. One estimate says Madagascar's population had been reduced by half by the time of her death. Some Malagasy did applaud the queen's return to old ways and her effort to end foreign influence. But those goals came at a very high price for the island nation.

# KING LEOPOLD II OF BELGIUM
## (1835–1909)

For several decades, the natural resources from a region of Africa called the Congo made King Leopold II of Belgium a rich man. In 1885, he had created a colony there called the Congo Free State. The colony did not belong to the country of Belgium. Rather, Leopold himself had bargained for and now owned the land and the precious resources it provided. But for the local Congolese people, there was no freedom in the Congo Free State. To get the rubber, ivory, and minerals from his colony, Leopold forced the Congolese to work for him and for the companies he allowed to operate there. The Congolese were, in reality, enslaved by Leopold.

Leopold's path to owning his own colony took several decades. (A colony is an area that is not governed by its native people but is under the control of another—often far distant—country.) He had been born in the Belgian capital of Brussels. His father, Leopold I, had become the first king of Belgium in 1831. The country had just won its independence from the Netherlands. Through his mother, Louise-Marie, young Leopold was related to the king of France.

As a member of such a royal family, Leopold learned how to speak German, French, and English. In school, though, he tended to be lazy. He began training to be a soldier when he was ten years old, and he joined the Belgian army as a teenager. By age twenty, he had earned the rank of major general. Leopold was never very close to his father. When the king wanted to tell his son something, he sent a secretary to deliver the message.

As a young man, Leopold married Marie-Henriette, a member of the royal family of Austria. The two were not in love—their families had arranged the marriage. Neither Leopold nor his wife were happy with the marriage. Having four children did not improve their situation. Leopold was not very fond of the nation he would one day rule, either. He once said Belgium was a small country with small (meaning unimportant) people.

Leopold became the king of Belgium in 1865. His tiny and still-young nation didn't control any foreign lands. But the larger, more powerful nations of Europe did. Leopold wanted a colony, too, thinking that would make Belgium look as powerful as the other European countries. He tried several times to buy existing colonies, but he couldn't find any sellers.

What he did find, though, was the large area in the center of the African continent called the Congo. Leopold claimed this land for himself. As he once said, "I do not want to miss a good chance of getting us a slice of this magnificent African cake." Like many white European rulers, Leopold believed he was entitled to claim less-developed foreign lands as his own.

In 1885, at a conference in Berlin, Germany, European leaders met to split most of Africa into colonies that would then be under their control.

No one from any African nation had any say in what would happen to their people, their lands, or their natural resources. The Europeans believed they were superior to any African and that they had a right to rule over them. Leopold told the other leaders in Berlin that he would bring the Christian faith to the Congolese. He said he would also expand trade with the region and end the slave trade there. With those promises, the European leaders agreed to give Leopold the land that became the Congo Free State.

Leopold had to spend his own money to build roads and railways to transport goods into and out of his new colony. He sometimes had to borrow cash to pay for all his efforts. His fortunes changed, though, when the world began to demand rubber. During the 1890s, bicycles became more popular, and cars were starting to appear on European and American roads. Both bikes and cars used rubber for their tires, and rubber was also used for tubes and other products. Soon, the Congo Free State was a major source of the world's rubber. It came from vines that grew in the tropical rain forest of the Congo.

The Congolese were forced to collect the rubber.

Men went into the jungle for days at a time. They didn't store the latex (the source of the rubber) that they collected in buckets or barrels; they covered their bodies with it and carried it out of the rain forest that way. They later scraped it off their skin, which was a painful process. While away collecting the latex, the men slept in cages to try to protect themselves from wild animals. If they did not collect enough latex, they might be whipped with a chicotte—a special whip that was made from the dried skin of a hippopotamus. It cut human flesh very deeply.

At times, the Belgians killed whole villages as a warning to other Congolese who did not want to collect rubber. Officers did not want their soldiers to waste bullets. So for every bullet the soldiers fired, they had to bring back a hand to prove they had killed someone. If they had used a bullet for hunting, some soldiers would then cut off the hand of a living person and claim they had used the bullet to kill a person.

The white European men who ran the companies and the government for the king treated the workers with horrific violence. Over about two decades, several million people in the Congo were killed or died from lack of food. Some historians think that between 1880 and 1920, half the population of the Congo was exterminated.

As he had promised in 1885, Leopold did send Christian missionaries to the Congo Free State. They were among the first people to report on the horrible and violent conditions there that helped make Leopold so wealthy. By the early 1900s, the world knew what Leopold was doing in his colony. The king dismissed the reports as lies. In 1906, he told a reporter that it made no sense for him to mistreat the Congolese. His colony could not prosper if they were unhappy.

But by then a British organization had formed to try to stop the horrors unfolding in the Congo. The public outcry led Leopold to form a commission to study the conditions there. He wanted it to say that all was well in the colony. But the investigators sent by the commission found more evidence of the violence that was so common in the Congo. In 1908, the country of Belgium took control of the Congo Free State. The Belgian government bought the colony from its king, only adding to his wealth. By one estimate, Leopold made more than $1 billion from the Congo Free State.

Leopold died in 1909. The Belgian colony of the Congo eventually became an independent country in 1960. It's known today as the Democratic Republic of the Congo. In Belgium, the country still has a king, a distant relative of Leopold II. Unlike in Leopold's day, the Belgian king has no real power. The country's government is run by lawmakers in parliament and a prime minister.

But the dark shadow of the power that Leopold once used so cruelly still haunts Belgium. Many young people in the country have demanded that Belgium recognize the horror Leopold caused in the Congo. Some statues of the king have been taken down, and some buildings named for him have been renamed. Belgians know they cannot continue to honor a man who bears the blame for the millions who were killed in the Congo.

# ADOLF HITLER
## (1889–1945)

Is one race of people or ethnic group somehow better than another? Is one group of people so superior to everyone else that they have a right to rule over others? And with that power, can they kill the people they consider inferior? The answer to all of these questions is, of course, "no."

Adolf Hitler believed some Germans were better than others. These "better" Germans formed what he considered to be a "master race" that Hitler hoped would rule most of Europe.

Other mass murderers of the twentieth century

killed even more people than Hitler and his government. Topping the list are Joseph Stalin of the Soviet Union and Mao Zedong of China. In those cases, some of the millions those leaders killed were their own people. But Hitler remains perhaps the greatest symbol of evil and extreme hatred in modern times, as he ordered the execution of millions of Jews and others during World War II.

The main targets of Hitler's hatred were the Jewish people of Germany who, for centuries, had been the targets of some European Christians. Hatred of Jewish people is called antisemitism. And it was not uncommon in Europe.

Antisemitism remained strong in Germany and other parts of Europe when Hitler was born in 1889. His family lived in Austria. Young Adolf spent time in Vienna, the country's capital, where early on he showed some of the traits that would emerge later in his life. His teachers described him as arrogant and easily angered. He believed he was smarter than other people, based on books he read on his own.

In Vienna, Hitler's hatred for the Jewish people began to grow. He read newspapers that spread antisemitic ideas. He began to believe that Jews were the cause of many social ills, such as some crimes. Hitler also believed that Jews spread political ideas he opposed, such as Marxism, an economic and political idea that opposes the ownership of private property.

As a young man, Adolf Hitler moved from Austria to Germany. When World War I began in 1914, he joined the German army. In November of 1918, Germany surrendered, ending the war. Hitler and other Germans came to believe that the country's Jewish citizens had played a major role in their defeat. They had called for peace. Then Germany had accepted harsh terms in the treaty that ended the war. Germany lost land to other European nations and had to get rid of its military. To Hitler and other antisemites (those who embrace antisemitism), the Jews had betrayed Germany. Hitler was determined to enter politics, rebuild Germany's strength, and punish the Jewish people.

Hitler's path to becoming a mass murderer started when he took over a German political party, founded by Martin Bormann, that today is known as the Nazi Party. Under Hitler, the party believed that Germany should seize lands belonging to other countries in Eastern Europe to give Germans "living space." They hoped to farm and set up industries in these new lands. The Nazi Party also shared Hitler's hatred of the Jews.

In elections held in 1932, the Nazi Party won more than two hundred seats in the Reichstag, the branch of the German government that wrote the country's laws. The Nazis controlled more seats than any other party. The next year, Hitler was named the chancellor of the government. In that role, he was the leader of the Reichstag. He and the Nazi Party now had control of the German government. Hitler did not wait long to put all his plans into action.

In 1933, Hitler began sending Jewish people and others he considered to be his enemies to special prisons called concentration camps. Along with the Jewish citizens, the camps held the Roma, gay people, and members of political parties Hitler disliked and distrusted. The prisoners, who had had no trials or legal hearings, had to work long hours for the government. Some were murdered.

The system of concentration camps grew as

Hitler and the Nazi Party carried out his plans to expand Germany's borders. First, he broke treaties by rebuilding the country's military. Then he sent his troops into neighboring Austria and Czechoslovakia. Finally, in 1939, his forces attacked Poland, launching World War II in Europe.

Over the next year, Nazi armies rolled through large parts of the continent. They built more prison camps, and some had gas chambers. Filling the chambers with poisonous gas made it easy to kill many people at one time. But many of the prisoners died slowly from starvation or harsh living and working conditions.

In 1942, Hitler began what he called "the Final Solution." This was his plan to exterminate the Jews of Europe. Jewish people living in regions the Nazi Party controlled were arrested and sent to new "death camps." Some stepped off the trains that brought them to the camps and were marched to the gas chambers. Some Jews were chosen to help carry out the murders, taking anything valuable the prisoners had, such as jewelry, then herding them into the chambers. These Jewish workers would eventually be gassed, too, with new prisoners taking their place. The gassings in the death camps went on through 1944. After that, many prisoners died from starvation or sickness.

German soldiers spread out across Europe, massacring Jews and others who tried to resist the Nazis. In Lithuania and elsewhere, local antisemites joined the Nazis in killing the Jewish people there.

The rest of the world knew about the death camps. But the true horror of what happened in them was not made clear until 1945, when US, British, and other forces fighting Germany found the camps and the mass graves. Adolf Hitler never faced trial for his genocide (his attempt to destroy an entire ethnic group) of the Jews and others. He died by suicide in Berlin in April 1945, right before the war's end.

An estimated six million Jews died because of Hitler's murderous policies. This mass killing is known today as the Holocaust. Others were also killed under Hitler's orders. They included almost two million civilians in Poland and millions more in the Soviet Union, which Germany had invaded in 1941.

Perhaps more than with any other mass murderer,

people today wonder what drove Hitler to kill so many. Why did he do what he did? There are no easy answers. His hatred of the Jewish people played a part. So did his sense that he was smarter than others. In his mind, he deserved to rule with absolute power. He believed he was meant to make Germany a supremely powerful nation.

Hitler is remembered as one of the most evil people to ever live. But he needed tens of thousands of others to help him carry out his Final Solution. Members of the Nazi Party, German citizens, and others obeyed his orders. Some did it gladly because they shared his antisemitism or his desire to expand German territory. Others did not want to face prison or death themselves. In either case, they served the goals of a truly deadly heart.

# IDI AMIN DADA
## (CA. 1925–2003)

What kind of man throws members of his own government into a lake filled with crocodiles? Or has an innocent seventy-three-year-old woman seized from her hospital bed and then murdered? Are these the actions of a madman? Or are they the methods used by a dictator who knows that ruling by fear makes it easier to stay in power? While Idi Amin Dada ruled the African nation of Uganda, some people said he was mentally ill. Others said he enjoyed having people think he was mad, so they would never know what he would do next.

When Amin was born, Uganda, in the central part of Africa and just to the north of Lake Victoria, was a British colony. Amin came from a poor family, and as a young man he joined the British Army and served as a cook. After a time, Amin left behind his pots and pans in Uganda and saw military action in neighboring Kenya. Although he was not well educated, Amin showed skills as a commander that impressed the British. They promoted him to the rank of lieutenant, which was rare for a Black Ugandan soldier. Helping Amin's rise was perhaps his imposing size. He stood six feet four inches tall, and later he earned the nickname "Big Daddy." Amin's towering size helped him become a boxing champion in Uganda during the 1950s.

In 1962, when Amin was in his late thirties, Uganda won its independence from the British. Amin continued to move up in the ranks in the new country's army. In 1966, he helped end a threat from a regional leader who opposed Uganda's national government. Over the years, Amin convinced himself that he had been the hero of a huge and bloody battle. In reality, his forces had easily defeated a small army. But in Amin's mind, his success on the battlefield meant he had been selected by God to do great things. Amin believed one day he would rise to be a great leader, and other world leaders would respect him. At times, he said, he received messages in dreams that told him what to do.

Amin was soon in charge of all of Uganda's military and police. With that power to support him, he seized control of the government in 1971. Uganda's population was made up of several different tribes. Those loyal to Amin began to attack soldiers who belonged to tribes that had supported the country's previous leader. During Amin's first year in power, he let these loyal soldiers kill about six thousand of the nine thousand men in the Ugandan army.

Killing enemies, real or imagined, became the heart of Amin's rule. He created several different police forces, which worked directly for him, to carry out these murders. Some victims were brought to prisons, where they were brutally tortured. Others might be found beheaded along the side of a road or stuffed in the trunk of a car. Amin used a special code to tell his police how to carry out his orders. When he said his men should go where someone sleeps, that meant the person should be killed. The order to give someone tea meant that they should be tortured and have their limbs cut off.

Not all of Amin's actions were deadly. Some were just cruel. Under British rule, thousands of people from India and Pakistan had come to Uganda to work. By the 1970s, their children and grandchildren owned many of the country's businesses. Amin said that in a dream, God told him to throw them out of the country. As many as fifty thousand people had to give up all they owned and flee Uganda. With these business owners and professionals gone, the country collected fewer taxes and so had less money to spend. Uganda grew poorer. Then Amin shut down elections in the country and controlled what the media said about him and his government.

Idi Amin seemed to be enjoying his reputation as a violent oppressor. When rumors spread that he had even killed and eaten one of his own sons, he didn't deny it! Amin said, "I don't like human flesh. It's too salty for me." Rumors also spread that he ordered the murder of one of his wives, though there is no proof of it.

Over his lifetime, Amin married six times.

During the eight years Amin was in power, he often insulted world leaders who criticized him. He called Julius Nyerere, the president of Tanzania, a coward. He said Henry Kissinger, an important US government official, was a murderer and a spy. He kept a list of people who were to be shot if they were ever found on a plane arriving in Uganda. In one of his most shocking comments, Amin said that Adolf Hitler had done the right thing by carrying out the Holocaust.

Interestingly, Amin actually had some supporters across Africa. They liked the way he insulted Europeans and other powerful whites who had controlled Africa for so long. In 1977, the British government removed its representatives from Uganda. Amin saw this as a defeat of Uganda's old colonial ruler. He gave himself a new title: conqueror of the British Empire. That name went along with another he had given himself—president for life.

International organizations who studied Amin's rule said he killed three hundred thousand or more Ugandans, many because of the country's tribal feuds.

Others were killed so the men who carried out Amin's deadly orders could take their land or other property. Some victims of the "Butcher of Uganda" were members of the government who had opposed Amin. It seemed that no one was safe from the tyrant's efforts to make sure he remained in power.

But in 1978, Amin finally made a move that led to his downfall. He sent troops into Tanzania, which borders Uganda. A combined force of Tanzanians and Ugandans who opposed Amin drove out the attackers and marched into Uganda. As these forces closed in on him, Amin fled the country. He traveled to Saudi Arabia, where he lived until his death in 2003, at around age seventy-eight. Amin never faced an international court or paid for his crimes.

Some people who knew Idi Amin thought mental illness drove his cruelty. Like some other deadly dictators, he believed he had been chosen by God to rule. That belief convinced Amin he could do anything to make sure he kept his power and his wealth.

# POL POT
## (1925–1998)

For the United States, the Vietnam War ended in April 1975. Over fifty-eight thousand Americans died in Vietnam and its surrounding countries, and more than three million Vietnamese died in the fighting. Devastation in the region, though, didn't stop in 1975. Events that started during the war eventually led to the mass killing of more than 1.5 million people in the nation of Cambodia, ordered by the country's own leader, Pol Pot. Why would he order the genocide of his own people? Pol Pot believed he was making Cambodia a paradise on Earth.

Pol Pot was the name Saloth Sar gave himself when he came to power. He came from a large family—he was one of nine children—and his parents were fairly wealthy farmers. When he was born, Cambodia was under French rule. He learned to speak French in school. As a young man, Pol Pot received money from the Cambodian government to study in France. There, he became interested in helping Cambodia win its independence from France.

While studying in France, Pol also learned about communism. Under this political system, the government owns most businesses and property. Only one political party controls the government, and most citizens do not have the right to free speech or to follow the religions they choose.

Pol Pot returned to Cambodia in 1953. The country won its independence that year, but it was a kingdom. Pol wanted Cambodia to have a communist government, and he helped start its first Communist Party. Vietnam, Cambodia's neighbor to the east, won its independence in 1954. Communists there also hoped to take over the government.

When the Vietnam War began in the 1950s,

Vietnam was divided into two countries. North Vietnam did have a communist government, and it wanted to control the south. The United States wanted South Vietnam to remain an independent nation. As the war there went on, Cambodia, to the west of Vietnam, was drawn into the fighting. Some South Vietnamese soldiers fighting for the north often fled into Cambodia to avoid US forces. These fighters and North Vietnamese troops also moved supplies through Cambodia. In 1969, President Richard Nixon began bombing the supply lines. The next year, he sent US troops into Cambodia.

During the 1960s, Pol spent time with rural tribes in Cambodia's hills. He began to think that the country should turn back to a simple way of life. Pol Pot thought Cambodia did not need merchants, scholars, and others who did not do physical work. He felt it would be best if people left the cities to work on farms.

The fighting that spilled over from the Vietnam War came at a time when Cambodia was in the middle of its own civil war. Pol Pot led a rebel group known as the Khmer Rouge. *Khmer* referred to an ancient kingdom that once thrived in the region. *Rouge* is French for "red." Red is the color of communism.

Starting around 1967, Pol Pot and the Khmer Rouge built a rebel army. After 1970, the United States government supported Cambodia's leader, Lon Nol. US bombing missions in the country killed tens of thousands of civilians. Pol Pot used the killings to convince Cambodians to join him in fighting Lon Nol. In 1975, the last remaining US troops in Cambodia left, and the Khmer Rouge defeated the troops who had been loyal to Lon Nol.

Among the communists in Cambodia, Pol Pot was known as Brother Number One. Before they came to power, members of the Khmer Rouge did not want the government to know their real names. So they called one another "brother" followed by a number. Being number one showed that Pol Pot was their leader.

As the new ruler of Cambodia, Pol Pot quickly began to carry out his plan for a new Cambodia. In 1976, he renamed the country Democratic Kampuchea and killed anyone he considered an enemy to his revolution. The dead included Lon Nol's soldiers—

even those who had surrendered—and the people who had worked in his government. Also targeted were Cambodian citizens with college educations, Buddhist monks, Muslims, and people originally from China or other foreign nations. Just being able to speak a foreign language could get someone arrested and tortured by the Khmer Rouge—even though Pol himself spoke French!

As the killings and arrests went on, Pol Pot forced people out of Cambodia's cities. He made them move to the country and become farmers, even children and patients in hospitals.

Everyone sent to the farms worked without pay, and soldiers stood guard to make sure they kept working. People in Cambodia were not allowed to own their own property or practice any religion. Under the harsh working conditions, hundreds of thousands of Cambodians died from starvation and disease. Many were buried in mass graves, which came to be known as the killing fields.

Pol Pot promised that his changes would make the country of Cambodia wealthier than it had ever been. But his policies included shutting the country off from the rest of the world. That meant it could not get foreign aid or advice. The country was not growing enough food for its people.

Pol Pot blamed members of his own party for some problems, and they became his victims, too. Many of the people he had arrested were sent to prisons called security centers. There, they were tortured and killed. The most notorious of the centers was Tuol Sleng. People held there were eventually executed and buried at a nearby killing field. On some days, as many as three hundred people might be taken from the prison and killed.

In person, Pol Pot was soft-spoken and a bit shy. One American journalist said he was elegant and polite. (After all, he had been well educated and had lived in Paris.) But underneath it all beat a deadly heart. Almost everyone agreed that he was convinced he had enemies everywhere—and a right to track down and kill those enemies.

The Khmer Rouge were forced from power in 1979. Over the years that followed, Pol Pot tried to fight his way back into power. He still wanted control of his country, which had formally changed its name to the State of Cambodia in 1989. In the end, former Khmer Rouge members turned against him. They forced him to remain in his home. He died in 1998 before he could go on trial for engineering one of the worst genocides the world has ever seen.

# SELECT BIBLIOGRAPHY

**\*Books for young readers**

\*Burgan, Michael. *Tyrants and Dictators: Stories of Ruthless Rulers*. Mankato, MN: Capstone Press, 2010.

De Madariaga, Isabel. *Ivan the Terrible: First Tsar of Russia*. New Haven, CT: Yale University Press, 2005.

Hochschild, Adam. *King Leopold's Ghost: A Story of Greed, Terror, and Heroism in Colonial Africa*. Boston: Mariner Books, 1998.

Kershaw, Ian. *Hitler: A Biography*. New York: W. W. Norton, 2008.

Klein, Shelley. *The Most Evil Dictators in History*. London: Michael O'Mara, 2004.

Laidler, Keith. *Female Caligula: Ranavalona, Madagascar's Mad Queen*. Rookhope, UK: Aziloth Books, 2016.

*Medina, Nico. *Who Was Genghis Khan?* New York: Penguin Workshop, 2014.

*Medina, Nico. *Who Was Julius Caesar?* New York: Penguin Workshop, 2014.

*Waterfield, Kathryn, and Robin Waterfield. *Who Was Alexander the Great?* New York: Penguin Workshop, 2016.